Birthday

words by Jill McDougall
illustrated by Bill Wood

"Have some hot dogs,"
said Bear.

3

"Slurp!" went Wolf.

And he ate them all up.

5

"Oh!" said Bear.
"No hot dogs left for us."

"Have some pancakes,"
said Bear.

7

"Slurp!" went Wolf.
And he ate them all up.

"Oh!" said Bear.
"No pancakes left for us."
"Have some peanuts,"
said Bear.

9

"Slurp!" went Wolf.
And he ate them all up.

10

"Oh!" said Bear.
"No peanuts left for us."

Wolf looked sick.

"Have some birthday cake," said Bear.

"Burp!" went Wolf.
"Oh, no! I'm full."

"Yum!" said Bear.
"Birthday cake for us!"

16